# THE ADVENTURES OF ROB & ROCKY
## THE WALK TO SCHOOL
### BOOK ONE

Copyright © 2018 by Robert Bo Chaney
All rights reserved. No part of this publication may be reproduced, distributed, or
transmitted in any form or by any means, including photocopying, recording, or other
electronic or mechanical methods, without the prior written permission of the publisher, except in the case of brief quotations embodied
in critical reviews and certain other noncommercial uses permitted by copyright law. For permission requests,
write to the publisher, addressed "Attention: Permissions Coordinator,"
at the address below.

Robert Bo Chaney
Email: robandrocky@gmail.com
TgosketchPress
Chicago, Illinois
www.tgosketch.com

To my lovely wife, Charo, and two beautiful sons, Robert and Rakim. Never let anything stand between you and your dreams!

TO SCHOOL EVERY DAY ROB AND ROCKY WOULD WALK,
AND HAVE CONVERSATIONS, THEY LOVED TO TALK.

ROB ASKED ROCKY ONE DAY CALMLY,
"WHEN YOU GROW UP, WHAT DO YOU WANT TO BE?"

Rocky stopped and thought of things he had seen.
After a minute responded "A rapper!
Their money is green."

Rob, who was wiser and had knowledge to share, said, "Rappers are cool, but there are more choices out there."

Rocky said, "Tell me what you would do?"
Rob replied, "First, there are options I would have to go through."

"A FIREFIGHTER, POLICE, I COULD EVEN BE A MAIL MAN, AND DELIVER MAIL."

"THEIR MONEY IS GREEN AND THEY ALL LIVE SWELL."

"i WOULD TELL YOU MORE, AND i KNOW MORE THAT ARE COOL.
BUT i WILL SAVE iT FOR OUR WALK AFTER SCHOOL."

## Questions For Discussion

How many kids walk to school?

Do you talk to your friends on the way to school?

What do you talk about?

What do you want to be when you grow up?

## Questions For Discussion

How many of you have thought of becoming a professional athlete, rapper, or some other entertainer?

What does it mean to be a professional?

What type of professional people have you seen so far?

What type of lives do you believe professionals live?

**Dolch Sight words included in The Adventure of Rob & Rocky**

A
Every
And
Would
Walk
One

Their
All
What
To
He
There
Green

## The Author:

Robert "Bo" Chaney was raised in the Englewood area of Chicago, Illinois. After graduating from Dunbar High School, he earned a Bachelor's Degree in Education from Rockford University and a Master's Degree in Education Administration from Northern Illinois University. His experience includes teaching in urban schools for five years and serving in the Rockford, Illinois fire service, currently in his 14th year. He discovered that there is a misconception circulating, that no one cares about our youth. As a result of his personal experiences as well as the interactions that he has had with today's young people, he has a passion for reaching as many young adults as he can. Throughout his adult life, Bo has successfully mentored many young, underserved, minority males, empowering them with the knowledge and skills to navigate school and the workplace. Bo has spent many hours developing a curriculum that is customized to meet the needs of underserved youth. Through his dedication, he's found ways to prepare young people for the workforce, through strategic lessons and connections which "uncover the unknown." He resides in Rockford, Illinois, with his wife, Charo and two sons. He enjoys spending time with his family, playing sports, coaching sports and traveling to new areas.

robandrocky@gmail.com
www.robandrocky.com

## The Illustrator:

Tyrus Goshay is an award-winning digital illustrator and 3D artist with over 18 years of experience. He serves as a college professor, teaching both game design and illustration in his off time. Tyrus has a Bachelor's in Computer Animation and Multimedia and a Master's in Teaching With Technology (MALT). He has contributed to several award-winning projects in the world of toy design and has been recognized for his achievements in academia as well. He also has tutorials in illustration and digital sculpting available on the web.

Visit his bookstore, and see other books that he has illustrated.

www.tgosketch.com
www.facebook.com/Tgosketch
tgosketch@gmail.com
Instagram/tgosketch

Made in the USA
Lexington, KY
17 August 2018